The Coral Reef

Photographs by Jerry Greenberg
Text by Idaz Greenberg

Contents

Printed in U.S.A. by H&D Graphics

The long look

Beyond the sun-dappled shallows lies
the world of the deep reef. In this
blue zone, from 25 to 60 feet deep,
only the diver freed from the surface
by a self-contained air supply can
glide effortlessly for a long look at
the intricate wonders of the reef.

Oasis in the sea

The coral reef is a splendid example of a balanced natural
habitat. Sea fans, anemones and sponges fasten onto the coral.
Crustacea dwell in the many nooks and recesses formed by the
coral heads. Small creatures find nourishment and haven among the
reef growths and in turn provide food for larger animals.
Each species of coral polyp has its own typical growth and
reproduction pattern, forming the various colonies we see in the
seascape above. Some corals branch out into tree-like shapes
while others form convoluted boulders.

The coral reef is an ancient association of life forms
that have been in existence 500 million years. Individual
coral polyps are tube-shaped and range in size from pinhead to
one foot across. The close-up of a colony (left) is four times
life-size. It shows the slit-like mouth opening surrounded
by tentacles that extend to sting and trap food. Cells on the
lower sides and bottom of this animal produce the limestone
that builds islands and reefs. The fringing reef (right)
is formed by literally billions of these tiny creatures

Coral is fed by water currents that bring it plankton, the
tiny organisms suspended in seawater that sustain even great
whales. Temperatures most favorable to vigorous growth range
from about 75° to 85° F. This need for warm water limits
most reefs to the eastern shores of continents in the
subtropic and tropic zones. Reef coral always has, living within
itself, small plant-like cells called zooxanthellae. Since
these organisms require light in order to live, reef corals are
generally found in water depths of less than one hundred feet.

Stone flowers: hard corals

Hard corals are the masons of the stone castles that make up the reef. Some colonies of polyps create fragile lacy clusters, while others build massive structures that reach the sea surface from depths of 35 feet.

9

Brain corals

Structural patterns of this coral resemble the meandering pathways of the human brain. Unlike the brain, the only living parts are on the surface. The polyp grows outward, enlarging the colony by budding and dividing until huge boulders are formed. Coral polyps are extremely long-lived, with a life span of centuries. The smaller brain coral *(Diploria labyrinthiformes)*, contrasts with the bolder convolutions of *Colpophyllia natans*, left and two times life-size below.

Pillar coral

Another name for *Dendrogyra cylindrus* is cathedral coral. These gothic spires are often inhabited by tiny fish with colors of stained glass. This rarely seen coral usually grows apart from the reef. The pillars are very sturdy, but the colony is slow-growing and does not cover a large area, which may account for its scarcity.

Staghorn coral

Though delicate and easily broken at the tips, staghorn coral *(Acropora cervicornis)* is an important reef builder. Like its relative the elkhorn coral, staghorn forms extensive underwater growths, but does not attain as great a height.

Feathers and fans: soft corals

The Gorgons of mythology had snakes for hair and visages so horrid that all who gazed upon them were turned to stone. Their namesakes, the gorgonians, include sea fans and whips. The skeletal structure is resilient and undulates, snakelike, with the movement of water around it.

Gorgonians

Flamboyant in shades of purple, orange, blue,
green and yellow, these plumes, whips and fans
are a conspicuous feature of the coral reef.
Soft corals belong to the same class
as hard corals, Anthozoa, but differ from them in many
ways. The flexible skeletal core is made up of
a tough, horny substance called gorgonin. Each
polyp has eight tentacles, as opposed to six or
multiples of six for hard corals. Food taken
in by any polyp is utilized by the whole
colony in its common digestive system, while
hard corals have individual stomachs. Gorgonians
occur at all depths. The brilliant orange-red
Iciligorgia schrammi (right) was photographed
at a depth of 90 feet, where it looked brown
until the flash revealed its glowing color.

Sea fans

Peacock-hued sea fans present themselves broadside to the prevailing current in order that each polyp may be exposed to a maximum number of food organisms. *Gorgonia ventalina* (left) has fastened its short main trunk firmly to a clump of *Porites astreoides.* The brilliant yellow and green *Gorgonia flabellum* (below) is usually found in shallow, surging water.

Plume worms

Concentric twin spirals of feathery gills mark the dwelling place of the serpulid plume worm. This distant relative of the common earthworm remains out of sight in its calcareous tube, permanently imbedded in coral. Only the vivid gill plumes extend outside the tube, to breathe and trap plankton. These plumes retract instantly at the threat of disturbance.

Seven times life-size (left) and twice life-size (above)

Sea filters:
the sponges

Though complex in appearance, sponges are simple, multi-celled animals equipped to filter vast quantities of water. Several hundred gallons per day may pass through a sponge in order for it to obtain food and oxygen. Sponges are found in all seas at all depths. They are difficult to identify because they vary in shape, size and color according to the substrate they fasten to and other local conditions. Barrel sponge *(Xestospongia muta)* left, is approximately five feet tall. Tube sponge *(Callyspongia plicifera)* below, is 16 inches high.

Reef tenants: the fishes

The fish that inhabit the reef are its greatest adornment. They glisten in the soft blue light as they parade by in bizarre, kaleidoscope dots and stripes, often as eccentric in behavior as appearance.

Parrotfish

An efficient recycling machine, the parrotfish turns coral and rock into fine sand in the process of grazing algae. Females and males often share a color pattern, but an occasional male attains larger size and more brilliant color and is called a terminal-phase male. The stoplight parrotfish *(Sparisoma viride)* below right, may be male or female, while its companion to the left is a terminal male of the same species, reaching about 20 inches. The terminal male redband parrotfish *(Sparisoma aurofrenatum)* left, is a smaller species, about ten inches in length.

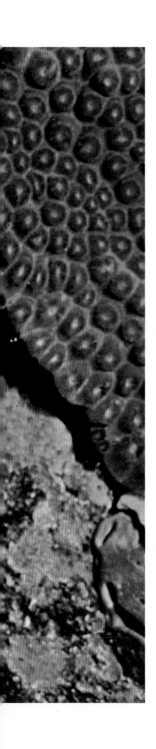

Angelfish

Garbed in a galaxy of colors, the
queen angelfish *(Holacanthus ciliaris)*
derives its imperial status from the
crown on its nape. The electric blue
that spots and rings the crown seems
to pulsate in brilliance. This
lavish coloring blends in surprisingly
well as it flutters among sea fans
or nibbles on bright-hued sponges that
are the mainstay of its diet.
Angelfish are the most curious and
least fearful fish on the reef. They
will hover within a few feet of a
diver, presenting an excellent
target for pictures. The immature
angels, marked with different color
patterns than the adults, are equally
photogenic. Angelfish may reach
a length of 18 inches.

Blue angelfish
Very similar to the queen
angel, the blue angelfish
(Holacanthus isabelita)
top, lacks its crown.

The French angelfish
(Pomacanthus paru) left,
is basically black with
yellow scalloping each
scale. The gray angelfish
(Pomacanthus arcuatus)
right, sports various
shades of velvety grays.
The boldly striped young
of these two species are
very similar, and only
in maturity are they
easily distinguished from
one another.

Groupers

The Nassau grouper *(Epinephelus striatus)* exhibits interesting characteristics common to many sea basses. All groupers mature first as females and produce eggs. They change sex later in life to become functioning males. Groupers can affect rapid color changes, going from light to dark in seconds. Nassau groupers may reach a size exceeding three feet in length.

Jewfish

Capable of providing enough food for a good-sized banquet,
this giant sea bass can be recognized by size alone.
The jewfish *(Epinephelus itajara)* may grow to
eight feet and weigh over 700 pounds.

Look, but don't touch!

Among the dangers to man in the sea, the most commonly hazardous are of a passive nature. Stinging corals and red fire sponge do not seek out man. If left undisturbed, the spotted scorpionfish *(Scorpaena plumieri)* sits quietly on the sea floor, preying upon small fish and crustacea that venture too near its well-camouflaged exterior. Divers should take care not to touch or step on scorpionfish, as puncture wounds from its spines can cause infection and great pain. Other creatures to be avoided are stingrays that often burrow in the sand, sea urchins and bristleworms.

Sea urchin

The long spined sea urchin *(Diadema antillarum)* has jet black spines that can penetrate human skin easily and break off, causing intense stinging pain.

Bristleworm

The decorative white bristles of *Hermodice carunculata* are its armament. These brittle lengths of glasslike matter detach with ease upon contact, and produce severe pain lasting several hours.

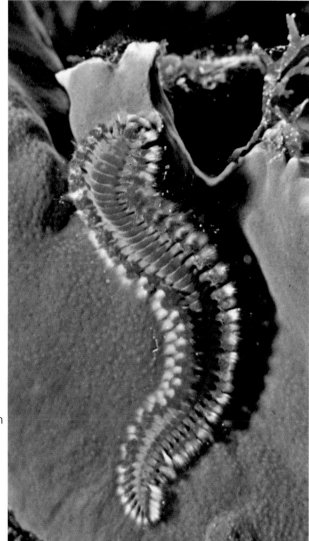

Though guilty of some attacks on humans in poor visibility situations or when speared, the great barracuda (*Sphyraena barracuda*) poses a more serious threat to the digestive tract when eaten than in the open sea. More ciguatera (fish poisoning) has been caused by barracuda than any other fish. These predators may reach a length exceeding six feet, but are seldom encountered more than four feet long.

Rogues' gallery

Shark

Sharks do not dwell on the reef, but, like the bull shark *(Carcharhinus leucas)* only visit occasionally. If divers do not kill fish, the danger posed by sharks may be minimized, as sharks are attracted to an area by the low frequency vibrations and scent trails from wounded fish.

Moray eels

As beautiful and repulsive as the snakes they resemble, these fish are largely nocturnal and secretive by nature. They are harmless to man unless provoked, hiding in crevices and under coral ledges. The goldentail moray *(Muraena miliaris)* left, grows to no more than two feet. The green moray *(Gymnothorax funebris)* below, has awesome teeth and is among the largest of eels, reaching a length of six feet and weight of 25 pounds.

Living jewels:
marine tropicals

Animated gems that flit about in their coral setting,
marine tropicals are the gaudy embellishment of the reef.
Copper sweepers *(Pempheris schomburgki)* add a metallic luster
to the caves and hollows they usually inhabit.

Squirrelfish

Poised over sponge-encrusted mound coral, the squirrelfish *(Holocentrus rufus)* right, is an impressive sight with its spines extended. Though most of the squirrelfish group are nocturnal, this species is active in the daytime, and is more commonly seen by reef divers. The dusky squirrelfish *(Holocentrus vexillarius)* top, emerges to feed at night. Light of day sends it into hiding in caves and crevices with other nocturnal fish, such as sweepers and bigeyes. *H. vexillarius* reaches a size of about six inches, half the length of *H. rufus.*

Damselfish

Small but pugnacious damselfish will nip at large fish
or even divers when their territory is threatened. The male
usually stands guard over the dark red to purple egg clusters
lest they be gobbled up by other fish. The sergeant major
(Abudefduf saxatilis) bottom right, abounds on the
reef. The yellowtail damselfish *(Microspathodon chrysurus)*
below, flashes its metallic blue spots as it browses algae
from dead coral surfaces. Both the sergeant major and the
yellowtail damselfish reach a maximum size of seven inches.
The cocoa damselfish *(Eupomacentrus variabilis)* top right,
rarely exceeds four inches in length.

Creole wrasse

Emblazoned with vivid shades of purple, the creole wrasse *(Clepticus parrai)* features an interior of pale blue teeth and bones. This fish attains a length of 10-12 inches.

Glasseye

Retiring beneath its daytime shelter, the glasseye snapper *(Priacanthus cruentatus)* is nocturnal. Shown life-size (left), this member of the bigeye family can grow to 12 inches.

Crustaceans

Crustaceans, like their terrestrial counterparts, the insects, have a hard exoskeleton. This protective covering derives rigidity from its lime content. The spiny lobster *(Panulirus argus)* top left, molts its old shell periodically in order to expand within the new covering, and reaches a length of over 20". The tail, that succulent reservoir of sweet meat, is composed largely of muscles used for backward propulsion. The banded coral shrimp *(Stenopus hispidus)* lower left, often performs grooming duties by eating parasites from the mouths of moray eels. This feeding ritual, coupled with its

barber pole stripes, probably accounts for its other common name, barber shrimp. The coral crab *(Carpilius corallinus)* this page, has powerful claws capable of crushing sea urchins and clams.

Squid and octopus

Enormous eyes remarkably like man's gleam through the water as waves of fluorescent colors pulse over the mantle of the popeyed squid *(Sepioteuthis sepioidea)*, top. Giant squid can reach two tons in weight and 60 feet in length, but this small reef species is about 15 inches long. Squid and octopus have a highly developed nervous system and intelligence superior to other marine life, excepting mammals. When frightened, they turn white, jet backwards by blasting water through a siphon in their mantle cavity, and squirt inky fluid to mask odor and distract the predator. *Octopus vulgaris* (right) often escapes danger by squeezing its boneless body through extremely small openings. Both the eight-footed octopus and its fellow cephalopod, the ten-footed squid, can regenerate lost sucker-studded tentacles.

55

Safety in numbers:
the schooling fish

Silvery schools of smallmouth grunts
(Haemulon chrysargyreum) are seldom found
more than a few yards from the reef by day.

Goatfish

Rarely exceeding a length of 15",
yellow goatfish *(Mulloidichthys
martinicus)* are nevertheless a
prized fishermen's catch for the
pot. Goatfish probe the sandy sea
floor with their long barbels
searching out small invertebrates
to feed on.

Grunts

Named for the sounds they are
able to produce, grunts hover over
the reef in huge schools during
the day. At night, they spread out
on the sand and grass flats to feed.
The white grunt *(Haemulon plumieri)*
can grow up to 16 inches long.

Porkfish

Dense, moving schools of fish make it hard for a predator
to single out one fish for attack. More than one genus may
school together. Porkfish *(Anisotremus virginicus)*, one-foot
long members of the grunt family, are usually found in
shallow inshore waters. *Chromis multilineatus,* in left
background, seems to find this an ideal living area as well.

Spadefish

Curious spadefish *(Chaetodipterus faber)*
swim a silvery circle about a diver.
This species average 15 inches long.